TRUMP

SACRIFICE AND STRENGTH

ISBN; 978-1-948680-65-3

July 13th, 2024: A Turning Point for America

On July 13th, 2024, a dark shadow fell over our nation as an assassination attempt was made on the life of President Donald Trump. In a moment that could have ended in tragedy, the President's life was spared by a mere second's turn of his head, a stroke of divine providence that averted disaster. This harrowing event has not only underscored the fragility of our times but also illuminated the urgent need for strong, decisive and unwavering leadership.

In the face of this unprecedented attack, President Trump stood unwavering, his resolve galvanized and his commitment to the American people stronger than ever. The image of him, fist raised in defiance and surrounded by Secret Service agents, has become a symbol of resilience and strength. It is a stark reminder of the sacrifices made by those who lead and protect our nation.

The attempt on President Trump's life is a call to action for all Americans. It highlights the pressing need for unity, security, and a collective commitment to uphold the values that make our country great. We are reminded that the journey towards a brighter future requires unwavering determination and the courage to confront challenges head-on.

The Need for Change

This event has exposed vulnerabilities that must be addressed to ensure the safety and prosperity of our nation. It is a stark reminder that complacency is not an option. We need robust policies and strategies to protect our leaders and safeguard our democracy. It is a time to re-evaluate our priorities and implement changes that reinforce the foundation of our great nation.

Strong Leadership for a Stronger Future
The bravery displayed by President Trump on that fateful day exemplifies the kind of leadership America needs. Strong, decisive, and unyielding in the face of adversity. It is this type of leadership that will guide us through turbulent times and towards a future of prosperity and security.

President Trump's resilience is a testament to his dedication to the American people. His ability to stand tall amidst threats and challenges is an inspiration to us all. It is a call to embrace the same spirit of perseverance and courage in our own lives.

July 13th, 2024: A Turning Point for America

Strong Leadership for a Stronger Future

The bravery displayed by President Trump on that fateful day exemplifies the kind of leadership America needs. Strong, decisive, and unyielding in the face of adversity. It is this type of leadership that will guide us through turbulent times and towards a future of prosperity and security.

President Trump's resilience is a testament to his dedication to the American people. His ability to stand tall amidst threats and challenges is an inspiration to us all. It is a call to embrace the same spirit of perseverance and courage in our own lives.

A Moment of Reflection and Action

As we reflect on the events of July 13th, let us honor the resilience and strength demonstrated by our President. Let us use this moment as a catalyst for positive change, uniting in our efforts to build a safer, stronger, and more prosperous America. This is not just a time to remember but a time to act, to ensure that the sacrifices made are not in vain and that our nation continues to thrive under strong and principled leadership.

In the face of adversity, let us find the strength to stand united, the resolve to implement necessary changes, and the courage to support the leaders who embody the true spirit of America. Together, we can ensure that the legacy of resilience and strength endures, guiding us towards a future where America remains a beacon of hope and freedom.

Date_____

_____
_____
_____
_____
_____
_____
_____
_____
_____
_____
_____
_____
_____
_____
_____
_____
_____
_____
_____
_____
_____
_____
_____
_____
_____
_____
_____
_____
_____
_____
_____

DATE_____

DATE_____

DATE_____

_____
_____
_____
_____
_____
_____
_____
_____
_____
_____
_____
_____
_____
_____
_____
_____
_____
_____
_____
_____
_____
_____
_____
_____
_____
_____
_____
_____
_____
_____
_____
_____

DATE_____

DATE_____

DATE_____

DATE_____

DATE_____

_____
_____
_____
_____
_____
_____
_____
_____
_____
_____
_____
_____
_____
_____
_____
_____
_____
_____
_____
_____
_____
_____
_____
_____
_____
_____
_____
_____
_____
_____
_____
_____
_____

DATE_____

DATE_____

DATE_____

DATE_____

DATE_____

DATE_____

_____
_____
_____
_____
_____
_____
_____
_____
_____
_____
_____
_____
_____
_____
_____
_____
_____
_____
_____
_____
_____
_____
_____
_____
_____
_____
_____
_____
_____
_____
_____
_____
_____

DATE_____

D<small>ATE</small>_____

DATE_____

DATE_____

DATE_____

DATE_____

DATE_____

D<small>ATE</small>_____

Date_____

PRESIDENT DONALD J TRUMP · UNITED STATES OF AMERICA

DATE_____

DATE_____

D<small>ATE</small>_____

DATE_____

_____
_____
_____
_____
_____
_____
_____
_____
_____
_____
_____
_____
_____
_____
_____
_____
_____
_____
_____
_____
_____
_____
_____
_____
_____
_____
_____
_____
_____
_____
_____

DATE_____

DATE_____

DATE_____

PRESIDENT DONALD J TRUMP
UNITED STATES OF AMERICA

DATE_____

_____
_____
_____
_____
_____
_____
_____
_____
_____
_____
_____
_____
_____
_____
_____
_____
_____
_____
_____
_____
_____
_____
_____
_____
_____
_____
_____
_____
_____

DATE_____

DATE_____

DATE_____

DATE_____

D<small>ATE</small>_____

DATE_____

_____
_____
_____
_____
_____
_____
_____
_____
_____
_____
_____
_____
_____
_____
_____
_____
_____
_____
_____
_____
_____
_____
_____
_____
_____
_____
_____
_____
_____
_____
_____
_____
_____
_____
_____
_____

DATE_____

DATE_____

DATE_____

DATE_____

DATE_____

D<small>ATE</small>_____

DATE_____

_____
_____
_____
_____
_____
_____
_____
_____
_____
_____
_____
_____
_____
_____
_____
_____
_____
_____
_____
_____
_____
_____
_____
_____
_____
_____
_____
_____
_____
_____
_____
_____
_____

DATE_____

DATE_____

DATE_____

DATE_____

_____
_____
_____
_____
_____
_____
_____
_____
_____
_____
_____
_____
_____
_____
_____
_____
_____
_____
_____
_____
_____
_____
_____
_____
_____
_____
_____
_____
_____
_____
_____
_____
_____
_____

DATE_____

DATE_____

DATE_____

_____
_____
_____
_____
_____
_____
_____
_____
_____
_____
_____
_____
_____
_____
_____
_____
_____
_____
_____
_____
_____
_____
_____
_____
_____
_____
_____
_____
_____
_____
_____

DATE_____

_____
_____
_____
_____
_____
_____
_____
_____
_____
_____
_____
_____
_____
_____
_____
_____
_____
_____
_____
_____
_____
_____
_____
_____
_____
_____
_____
_____
_____
_____

DATE_____

DATE_____

DATE_____

D<small>ATE</small>_____

DATE_____

DATE_____

DATE_____

DATE_____

DATE_____

Date_____

DATE_____

DATE_____

DATE_____

DATE_____

DATE_____

Date_____

DATE_____

DATE_____

DATE_____

DATE_____

DATE_____

Date_____

DATE_____

DATE_____

DATE_____

DATE_____

DATE_____

_____
_____
_____
_____
_____
_____
_____
_____
_____
_____
_____
_____
_____
_____
_____
_____
_____
_____
_____
_____
_____
_____
_____
_____
_____
_____
_____
_____
_____
_____
_____
_____

DATE_____

DATE_____

DATE_____

DATE_____

_____
_____
_____
_____
_____
_____
_____
_____
_____
_____
_____
_____
_____
_____
_____
_____
_____
_____
_____
_____
_____
_____
_____
_____
_____
_____
_____
_____
_____
_____
_____

DATE_____

DATE_____

DATE_____

DATE_____

_____
_____
_____
_____
_____
_____
_____
_____
_____
_____
_____
_____
_____
_____
_____
_____
_____
_____
_____
_____
_____
_____
_____
_____
_____
_____
_____
_____
_____
_____
_____

DATE_____

DATE_____

_____
_____
_____
_____
_____
_____
_____
_____
_____
_____
_____
_____
_____
_____
_____
_____
_____
_____
_____
_____
_____
_____
_____
_____
_____
_____
_____
_____
_____
_____
_____
_____

Date_____

_____
_____
_____
_____
_____
_____
_____
_____
_____
_____
_____
_____
_____
_____
_____
_____
_____
_____
_____
_____
_____
_____
_____
_____
_____
_____
_____
_____
_____
_____
_____

DATE_____

Date_____

DATE_____

DATE_____

_____
_____
_____
_____
_____
_____
_____
_____
_____
_____
_____
_____
_____
_____
_____
_____
_____
_____
_____
_____
_____
_____
_____
_____
_____
_____
_____
_____
_____
_____
_____

DATE_____

Date_____

DATE_____

DATE_____

DATE_____

_____
_____
_____
_____
_____
_____
_____
_____
_____
_____
_____
_____
_____
_____
_____
_____
_____
_____
_____
_____
_____
_____
_____
_____
_____
_____
_____
_____
_____
_____
_____

DATE_____

DATE_____

DATE_____

DATE_____

_____
_____
_____
_____
_____
_____
_____
_____
_____
_____
_____
_____
_____
_____
_____
_____
_____
_____
_____
_____
_____
_____
_____
_____
_____
_____
_____
_____
_____
_____

Date_____

Date_____

DATE_____

_____
_____
_____
_____
_____
_____
_____
_____
_____
_____
_____
_____
_____
_____
_____
_____
_____
_____
_____
_____
_____
_____
_____
_____
_____
_____
_____
_____
_____
_____
_____
_____

DATE_____

DATE_____

DATE_____

Date_____

DATE_____

Date_____

DATE_____

_____
_____
_____
_____
_____
_____
_____
_____
_____
_____
_____
_____
_____
_____
_____
_____
_____
_____
_____
_____
_____
_____
_____
_____
_____
_____
_____
_____
_____
_____
_____
_____
_____

Date_____

DATE_____

Made in the USA
Las Vegas, NV
19 December 2024

14923704R00070